THE FACE OF AMERICA

SAN FRANCISCO
WEST COAST METROPOLIS

BY

EDWIN ROSSKAM

With an Introduction by

WILLIAM SAROYAN

ALLIANCE BOOK CORPORATION

LONGMANS, GREEN AND COMPANY

NEW YORK · TORONTO

CONTENTS

INTRODUCTION

By William Saroyan

San Francisco is the genius of American cities. It is the wild-eyed, all-fired, hard-boiled, tender-hearted, white-haired boy of the American family of cities. It is the prodigal son. The city which does everything and is always forgiven, because of its great heart, its gentle smile, its roaring laughter, its mysterious and magnificent personality.

It is not the easiest city in the world to like at first. It seems cold, hard, ugly, indifferent, and out of the world. It is not an easy city to know. It seems delirious with energy, incoherent because of the many things it has to say, brokenhearted with sorrowful memories. You walk through the streets of the city and feel its loneliness, and you wonder what memory is troubling its heart. You step into a honky-tonk for a beer, and look at the people. Instead of being tramps as you'd imagine they would be in a honky-tonk, they're all good people. Two young men and two young women come into the place from Nob Hill. They're not slumming. They like the honky-tonk as much as they like the bar at the Mark Hopkins or at the Fairmont.

The city *is* cold. It *is* hard. It *is* ugly. It *is* indifferent. But at the same time it is also warmer than any other city; it is gentler; it is more beautiful; and it is kindlier.

It is an easy-going city. It is truly democratic. Within its narrow borders it houses any number of small worlds. Worlds of races, as well as worlds of classes. There is the whole Chinese world of Chinatown. The Italian world of the North Beach. The Russian world South of Market. The Negro world around Sutter and Fillmore.

v

The city enlarges the spirit, educates the heart, deepens the experience of living. It has all the virtues and all the vices. It is as little proud of one as it is ashamed of the other. It does not pretend to be anything it isn't. Brought into the world recklessly. Brought up recklessly. And now recklessly alive. Strong, hearty, heedless, bawdy, and human. A city with its head in the clouds and its feet in the valleys. A city humming a song of land and sea, of fog and blue skies, of ships and locomotives, hills and narrow winding streets, houses with melancholy faces and gay hearts, a song of youth and age, loneliness and delight, misery and mirth.

Every city is a world of some sort. San Francisco is *the whole world* recreated as a single work of art: a painting, a work of sculpture, a poem, a symphony, a story. It is the whole world brought together for the eye of man to behold and the heart to understand. It is all the nations of the world brought together in time and place, to test mortality. To see whether the experiment can be successful. To see if fraternity and brotherhood among the living is possible. In San Francisco there is only one race. The race of the living.

The city has the temperament of genius. It is unpredictable. Any street is liable to leap upwards at any time. The very weather is liable to change from winter gloom to spring warmth in ten minutes. Any building is liable to break out into a big smile at any moment and suddenly seem no longer ugly but beautiful. At least comically beautiful. It is a city with no rules. Like nature itself it improvises as it goes along. It does what it needs to do at the time and under the circumstances. It feels as it must feel at the time and under the circumstances. It is a sombre city, but it is a city with no regrets. It is a city with a soul, but it knows the value of pure physical sport.

San Francisco can be whatever you yourself wish it to be. It will not drive you to beautiful ruin unless you yourself are in the mood to go to beautiful ruin. It will run amok if you want it to; it will be as gentle as a cow if you want it to. Every person in San Francisco inhabits and knows his own San Francisco, just as every reader of Shakespeare reads and knows his own Shakespeare. The stranger coming to San Francisco has no alternative but to be an adventurer. No city in the world shines with greater promise. No city invites the heart to come to life as San Francisco does. Arrival in San Francisco is an experience of living. It is like a glass of champagne from a bottle that can never be emptied. The bottle is always there for you to drink from. Drink wisely or drink foolishly, as you prefer.

It is an unreasonable city. It makes friends of thieves, and ignores saints. And the next minute it punishes the thieves and opens its arms to the saints. But only for a moment. It soon returns to the thieves and abandons the saints. It loves the good as well as the evil. It is unfaithful to both. It makes enemies of everybody and it loves everybody.

The Pacific has a lot to do with the temperament of San Francisco. The city is literally of the sea. It has everything. Sea, earth, sky, and the world. And the wonderful people of the world. At The Sea Cliff you can sit at a table for a cup of coffee and from high up look out at the great, magnificent, lonely, lovely Pacific. Coffee never tasted better than that coffee, no matter what brand it happens to be. And a beautiful woman never seemed more beautiful than the one across the table from you, with the Pacific close and far-away.

There are no end of ways of enduring time in San Francisco, pleasantly, beautifully, and with the romance of living in everything. Eat any kind of dish the races of the world know how to prepare. Drink any kind of wine you like. Play any game you care to play. Go to the opera. The symphony. The concert. Go to a movie or a stage play. Loaf around in the high-toned bars, or in the honky-tonks. Sail in the bay. Go down to Bay Meadows or Tanforan and bet the horses. Go to church.

If you're alive, you can't be bored in San Francisco. If you're not alive, San Francisco will bring you to life. You may be a fool for a week or two, but nobody will notice that because everybody else has been a fool too, and is likely to be a fool again.

San Francisco is a world to explore. It is a place where the heart can go on a delightful adventure. It is a city in which the spirit can know refreshment every day.

There's no use telling you where to go in San Francisco. Avoid the guides. Go alone and find out for yourself. You'll have more fun. If a young man holds you up, tell him you just arrived in town. He'll put away his water-pistol and go drinking with you. Stranger, he'll say. This is a great town. One thing we haven't got in San Francisco is thieves. Myself, I'm an unemployed piano mover. People ain't moving pianos any more. All I wanted was three dollars anyway. Two for beer and one for a small present for my wife. We've been having a little bad luck. Nothing serious.

Go alone; nobody's inhuman in San Francisco. Have yourself an adventure in heaven, in the beautiful and ugly heaven that is San Francisco.

AUTHOR'S PREFACE

This book intends to use the combined medium of words and pictures to interpret a city. It is not a guide book. A hundred different sights and aspects, important no doubt in themselves, remain excluded because they do not help—in my opinion—to tell the story I here wish to tell: the story of one of America's vital cities, its functioning and its people.

I want to acknowledge, from the very start, the generous help I have received from so many quarters. Californians Incorporated, put at our disposal their invaluable experience and the fruits of their research. Such experts in their fields as Albert Bender, Ottorino Ronchi, David Chin, Paul Radin, George West and many others made this book possible.

But more than anyone I want to thank my wife, Louise Rosskam, who did all of the dirty work, the developing of negatives, the classifying, the note-taking and some of the photography. If this book is anything at all, she must have the credit. She was at my side at all times, fought with me over ideas until, in her constructive opposition, they crystallized into workable projects. In more ways than one she made this book.

GOLD COMES OF AGE

San Francisco was born out of gold-hunger and nursed on catastrophes. Today it lives, a little more sedately, on lettuce and ships, peas and silk, wine and scrap iron, dried fruits and bonds, walnuts and stocks, artichokes and mortgages. It is essentially a clearing house and a banking center, sitting, with its face toward the Pacific, on one of the richest agricultural lowlands of the world.

Martin Behrman Collection

1846

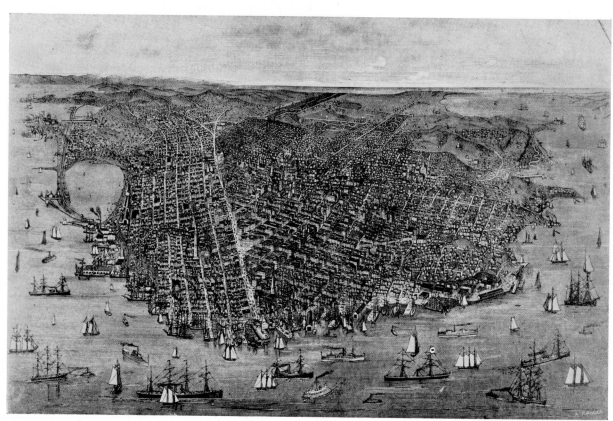

Martin Behrman Collection

1882

1939

San Francisco exploded into being. In 1847 there was a trading post with 459 residents . . .

Gold was discovered in 1848.

40,000 immigrants landed in 1849, put up their tents, had their brawls and struck out for the mines.

The population at this time staggered somewhere around 20,000. Estimates were, at best, approximations, because even the sailors of the ships and the soldiers of the army deserted for the interior. By 1852, when the worst of the scramble was over, there, suddenly, was a city of 40,000 souls.

A city there was—but what a city. Most of the houses were of wood and, after a rain, most of the streets were of mud. In this

Martin Behrman Collection

14

environment history was compressed so that calamities became commonplace. Fires swept the town periodically. Gangs of criminals established a reign of terror and were eliminated by terror. Depressions came and went. But fortune was a gambling wench beckoning to every man. Her reputation persisted long after she had settled down to a life of ease with the right people.

The city was a parvenu. In the best newly-rich tradition it exulted in show. Gentlemen of quality, just like their European contemporaries, fought duels; in San Francisco they advertised them beforehand in the newspapers. Palaces—wooden ones—enclosed by shiny brass fences, mushroomed fantastically.

In 1906 the whole shebang burned down. After the earthquake and fire the world press wrote the funeral oration of what seemed a cremated city. The eulogy was premature. The present San Francisco, with 730,000 inhabitants, is a thriving town, and this time, a lot of it is built of stone.

ARCHITECTURAL BEAUTIES

If you want to get an idea of San Francisco B. F. (before the fire), go west of Van Ness Avenue. Here you will still see them, those masterpieces of the cornice maker's art, left over from the time when wood took the place of stone and an empty wall was considered

an abomination. Here they age, their dead wood growing brittle, apotheoses of the curlicue, conglomerates of the bay window, the Moorish arch, and all the decorative patterns invented by humanity since the word go. Beside the latest functionalist fronts—their district is still fashionable—they stand as monuments to the mortality of human taste, before the ageless vista of the bay.

17

MISSION DOLORES

The Mission Dolores was founded in 1776 as the sixth of a series established, under the rule of Spain, by Father Junipero Serra. It is the only church in the city which remains intact from the earliest time of the Spaniards.

Mission Dolores is more familiar to out-of-towners than to natives. It is still used for three or four services during the year and a couple of marriages. But the building from which the

Indian life of a whole countryside was once controlled and from which a ranch with 100,-000 head of cattle was run, has degenerated to a stop-off place for rubberneck buses. . . .

"Ladies and gentlemen—the corner stone of the present church was laid by Father Palou April 25th, 1782, it is 114 feet long, 22 feet wide and its walls are four foot thick, you can look for yourself. The roof, ladies and gentlemen, has not got a nail in it, the timbers were lashed together with hide and were painted by the Indians, you can see for yourself how crude they are. The altar, all carved by hand and the statues were brought from Mexico in 1780. The bells are the originals and they are so old they have lost their tone, you will please follow me to the cemetery. . . ."

A statue of Father Serra stands, pensively, in the little graveyard beside the mission. Most of the weatherbeaten headstones are from the tragi-comic period of San Francisco's past, when it was trying, strenuously, to be adult while it was merely big for its age. Among the lovely flowers and shrubs, are the tombs of Casey and Cora, members of the criminal set of '56 who were hanged by the Vigilance Committee of citizens. The gravestone of James (Yankee) Sullivan, a gentleman of lesser prominence but of similar inclinations, testifies: "Died by the hands of the V.C."

There are early headstones of every kind of man under the purple heliotrope. The population of this cemetery is as international as the live city throbbing through the streets outside the walls. Spaniards of official rank, French adventurers, Russian sailors, and many Irish lie here. The inscriptions speak of peace and, in general, give no indication of the violence of the lives and deaths which now have become mere names. Only Casey, on his tomb decorated with firemen's helmets, threatens: "May God forgive my persecutors."

21

UPS

The inhabitants of San Francisco live, quite literally, on top of each other. Pedestrians, in the residential quarters especially, don't walk; they climb.

AND DOWNS

Driving a car around this town is a special accomplishment. Going up hill is comparatively simple—if you get a flying start and your clutch doesn't slip when your engine races in low. Coming down the darn things, for out of town drivers at least, is a matter of brakes and prayer: on wet days, prayer only. San Franciscans take it all with nonchalance, including the parking which is, as you can see, a cockeyed business.

Don't be shocked if the pavement makes funny
noises under your feet. It's only the cable which ties
the hills together. Don't think there's a fire if bells
jangle at you. The chances are it's only one of the
cable cars. As squat as bugs and as yappy as fox ter-
riers, these funny little boxes on wheels will bump
you over the steepest hills at nine miles an hour.
Don't miss a cable car ride. It's an experience. And
the turntable at the end of the line, operated by
hand, is old time vaudeville.

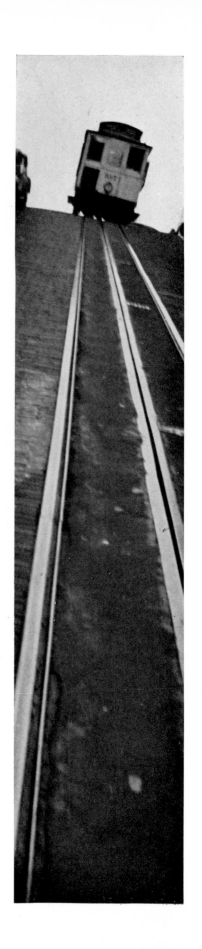

TELEGRAPH HILL AND COIT TOWER

San Francisco is a city of views surrounded on three sides by water. In the "to let" columns of the newspapers, views are advertised together with the plumbing, the refrigerator and the latest kitchen ranges.

Though Nob-hillers would probably slay anybody who says so, Telegraph Hill has the edge on the rest, historically speaking. As early as 1849 it had a signal station on its top which announced to the town at large the nature of approaching vessels. The signal denoting mail steamers usually caused a complete stoppage of work and a near-riot. It can thus be stated that Telegraph Hill was a functional part of San Francisco at a time when Messers Sweeny and Baugh, the signal men, were its only occupants.

Large chunks of Telegraph Hill are now under the waters of the harbor, and a lot of it has been lost, just lost. As the city expanded, there was need for more room to put warehouses, and business houses. The side of the hill was quarried out and dropped neatly into the bay, together with some old hulks, to create that whole section of town on the other side of Montgomery street. A considerable portion of the hill travelled around the Horn, ballasting ships which came carrying cargo and went back with nothing but cash and bank drafts.

Before the hill was thus dismantled, its slippery and inaccessible sides were peopled by as sterling a collection of convicts and hoodlums as were ever to populate Alcatraz. From here issued the raids and depredations which so annoyed the more respectable citizenry that the substantial end of town got together and did its own hanging.

Since then, anticlimactically, but quite naturally, the hill has developed into an artists' quarter with painters and sculptors enjoying the incredible vista from the little one-or-two-story wooden shacks that dot the steep slope. Like many other artists' quarters before, it is now succumbing to the longing for Bohemia by those whose incomes permit them to be comfortably daring. It is well on the way to becoming smart.

THE 1939 EXPOSITION FROM TELEGRAPH HILL

RUSSIAN HILL

Russian Hill, which got its name from a long vanished Russian burial ground, is so extensive that it cannot be summed up in a single phrase. Sections of it have apartment houses; other sections, criss-crossed with little alleys, are remote as country lanes in the middle of the metropolis. Like Telegraph Hill, it has attracted part of the intelligentsia but it is equally fashionable with business executives.

Its streets are the steepest in town. Among them, unique, the Lombard Street descent is as curved as a scenic railway.

There is a little story from that terrible April morning of 1906 when the fire was sweeping the city, that seems to sum up the spirit of the whole place. Writes James Hopper: "Upon the top of Jones Street hill, in the middle of the

28

street, the only thing standing in that direction for miles was a piano. A man was playing upon it. I could see his hands rising and falling, his body swaying. In the wind his long black hair and loosened tie streamed. The wind bore the sounds away from me, but in a lull I finally heard the music. It was Saint-Saëns's 'Danse Macabre' . . ."

NOB HILL

The Big Four—Crocker, Huntington, Stanford and Hopkins—made Nob Hill what it is and, involuntarily, gave it its name. They were the kings of California in their day and were admired and resented as such. According to different versions, the name of the hill is a contraction from either "Snob Hill" or "Nabob Hill."

In the effulgent fashion of their time, the "Nabobs" built mansions large enough to serve as barracks, elaborate enough to turn the stomach of a Maharajah. Unhappily, the disaster of 1906 had no respect for kings and millionaires. All that is left of these proud palaces is the tradition which still makes Nob Hill the swankiest and most expensive place to live. A modern hotel—also very-very—bearing Mark Hopkins' name, stands on the site of Mrs. Hopkins' dream of glory.

30

POTRERO

Potrero Hill is the reverse of Nob Hill. With a view of the city second only to the panorama from Twin Peaks, it is unfamiliar to San Francisco's upper crust. It is the hill of little people, not a boarding house district like the Mission, but rather the location where small home owners—shipyard workers, waterfront workers, and factory workers—raise chickens and hang up their laundry against a magnificent backdrop. Undoubtedly, the surrounding

warehouses and the smells of slaughter from Butchertown (when the wind is wrong) have kept the world of fashion, art, and wealth on the other side of the valley.

To a large extent, the hill is inhabited by people of foreign antecedents. Russians, Slovenians, Greeks, and many other nationalities in lesser numbers, live here, keeping intact the customs from the old country which spell home.

Adolph Sutro had the civic spirit. Dear to his 19th century German heart were the cultural values, which he tried his best, as Mayor, to graft upon the rowdy city. Appreciative of the finer things, he gave to San Francisco a grove of eucalyptus trees and a company of statues (made of plaster for economy, painted white for beauty). Upon a solid basis of Comstock silver he erected his mansion. With a wide tolerance characteristic of the man and his time, he selected his statuary: Venuses of Milo (2), Apollos, gnomes around the fountain, a one-winged Griffon, and two dark guardians of the gate in armor.

The park is open to the people now and has been so for a long time. They hold hands beside a paint-encrusted Leda, look out over the magnificent view of the beach underneath the Juno whose ample draperies have been slipping from equally ample hips for fifty years.

SUTRO HEIGHTS

FOG

The fogs of San Francisco are unpredictable. Through the Golden Gate or over the hills of Marin County, they roll without warning and spread between the bay and the bright daylight, between the hills and the morning. Sometimes they are thin layers, and the bridge towers project above them. Sometimes they are heavy and opaque, and envelop the city.

These mists are not weather; they are floating islands in the weather. One moment you may be over them. A minute later they will be wrapped around you. They're here, and then there, and then somewhere else. They tear apart and consolidate again while your head is turned. They are the very devil to photograph. To make the picture on the right, a view familiar to every San Franciscan, we had to chase the will-of-the-wisp in an automobile throughout an afternoon, only to lose it as we opened the camera. After an hour's waiting, with the trigger set, we finally caught it just before sunset.

The fogs of San Francisco have many voices. They hoot and howl and they blow sirens.

They play strange tricks with distance. It is not unusual to wake up and to find a steamer blowing on your roof. You are sure then, as you lie in your bed, that some doggone boat has lost its way and has climbed the hill and is sitting on top of the house, yelling like nightmare.

You go out in the street and the hills have gained infinity. The pavement under your feet goes off into a canyon without bottom. Haloes instead of street lamps, great rings of light with blurred centers, burn vaguely.

Shadows creep past you, out of obscurity into obscurity. And the way in which the automobiles crawl, makes you feel certain that they have grown feelers.

Fogs have a bad name in most places. But San Franciscans seem to appreciate their own. You can see them on any foggy Sunday, in troops, on the vantage points of Telegraph Hill or the Marina, watching the convolutions of the mist, the discovering and recovering of familiar sights.

Summer is the time of the densest and longest fogs. In July, August and September, the bay area is isolated from the broiling California heat of the agricultural valleys. San Franciscans complain when, at noon, the thermometer soars as high as eighty from its customary fifties. This creates a strange paradox. In the summer time, the wealthy people of the city go away to their country homes—to keep warm.

These pictures explain why engineers used to consider a bridge across the Golden Gate impossible. So swift are the currents and so strong the waves that the first massive fender for the pier on the San Francisco side was carried out bodily to sea.

The mountains in the background dwarf the world's tallest bridge towers and the world's longest span, and make a gigantic structure look almost dainty.

GOLDEN GATE BRIDGE

THE BAY BRIDGE

To San Franciscans, their bridges are dramatic events closer to their hearts than mere transportation carriers. Ever since Oakland and Berkeley grew up across the bay, men have been dreaming of a bridge to span it. The accomplishment of an ambition dear to an entire city's ancestry has made this bridge—which can be seen from at least two thirds of the town—a landmark as beloved by San Franciscans as is St. Paul's by Londoners.

Eight and a half miles in length, the bridge crosses in two suspensions to Yerba Buena Island; after tunnelling through the Island, it continues as a cantilever bridge to the other shore. Both structures are high enough to spare headroom for the "Normandie."

In January, 1939, with pomp and sentiment, San Franciscans bade farewell to the ferry boats which until then had carried commuters. Now you travel in swift electric trains. Breath-taking views flit by you at a speed gratifying to your American time-sense; if, however, you have a taste for panoramas, you may wish for engine trouble.

CIVIC CENTER

Right in the middle of town, there rises a $26,000,000.00 island of civic architecture. It contains the City Hall, the Federal Building, the Civic Auditorium, the Opera, the Public Library, et al. It is constructed in that peculiar hybrid style which has spread out from Washington all over the country, a style calculated to affirm in the façade a civic virtue presumably contained.

The picture below has caught one little scene, very characteristic of this city's spirit. Little kids go fishing in the monumental fountains. Note: they really catch fish, minnows put in there, we imagine, to keep mosquitoes out.

San Francisco has always been crazy about music and the stage. The gold rush was a great equalizer. Men of culture dug and panned shoulder to shoulder with the illiterate. When sidewalks were still made of packing boxes, Shakespearean plays were not unusual. Out of such a tradition, the city has acquired its own opera house. It assesses its tax payers to supplement the receipts of the San Francisco Symphony Orchestra. The result is a long music season at popular prices.

MARKET STREET

From the Ferry Building to Twin Peaks, Market Street cuts across town with a will of its own. Oblivious of intersections, it slices through the city's plan, parallel to nothing in particular and at sharp angles to the side streets.

It is "Main Street" gone big city. Boisterous, crowded, it swarms with restaurants and stores of the less expensive kind. Several blocks snap with the neon signs of movies, bars and hash houses.

The foot and the middle of the street are cosmopolitan and democratic. The shopping crowds and the movie crowds are drawn kaleidoscopically from bums and bankers, stenographers out for a quick lunch, mothers buying socks for their kids in the five and dime, and employees riding to and from work hanging like bunches of grapes from the overcrowded streetcars.

44

Market Street is the only thoroughfare we ever came across, on which the trolley cars seem to march four abreast. The city owns one line, a private company the other, and the fight between them has long been a headline controversy. The competing cars always run neck and neck, which is disconcerting to the out-of-towner who sees them bearing down upon him for the first time.

FINANCE

The history of San Franciscan finance is the history of California. Montgomery Street was the business center from the first, when the ships of the 49'ers landed to face emporiums and saloons, housed in shacks across a thoroughfare of mud. From here, the eager miners were outfitted by those who, understanding the transience of all booms, set out to hoard—in the concrete form of gold dust—the desperate long shot of a whole migration in search of miracle. A decade later, the mirage evaporated. But in the strong boxes of the Montgomery Street traders lay the solid cash.

Now they began to invest. They formed pools and companies, dug mines far underground, and built stable fortunes upon the gambles of their stockholders. Out of the ranks of the traders also grew the first great monopoly of California—the railroad. The Big Four started in Sacramento as four shopkeepers. To be financiers, they had to move to San Francisco.

The position of the city as a perfect harbor, centrally located, made it the inescapable magnet for all large scale operation. It also made it, inevitably, the coagulation point for the forces of labor.

It is impossible to consider the growth of one without the other. During the gold rush, when every tramp was a potential millionaire, even the common laborer got the taste of high wages. When the boom collapsed, wages collapsed. And while the Big Four, ostensibly building a railroad, put the state in their pocket, the craftsmen and mechanics and carpenters organized. Thus, while the territory was hardly more than a frontier, the cleavage between the Haves and the Have-nots was already more clear-cut than in the older and more industrialized East.

This situation has been intensified with the years. While the financial leaders of San Francisco added to a vast empire of transportation and public utilities an agricultural

empire larger than all the New England states, they learned to coordinate their forces. Here, the various branches of banking, industry, and agriculture forgot their diversified interests early, banded together in a series of continually perfected committees of strategy and, as early as 1916, broke the power of the unions. The revival of the union movement, stimulated in 1933 by the enactment of N.R.A., resulted in a forever closer cooperation between the different sections of capital. At present, Montgomery Street expresses itself through the Employers' Council, a federation of highly specialized employer groups. The Associated Farmers, a state-wide organization led from Montgomery Street, is the agricultural companion piece.

This, then, is the center. From here, the invisible threads reach out over the state and beyond its borders to Nevada and Oregon to control, tightly, an enormous wealth, the transportation of that wealth and its distribution.

THE EARLY BROKER CATCHES THE STOCK

Pity the poor broker! He must get up in the morning. In the dead of night, he must leave his country home down on the Peninsula and drive through the cold, raw dawn to arrive on the floor, at six in the summer and at seven during the rest of the year.

It's all the fault of geography and daylight saving. Modern science notwithstanding, the sun still takes three hours to cross the continent. And the San Francisco Stock Exchange, however important it may be in itself, still remains the vassal of Wall Street.

According to custom, broker picks up broker in a lowly station wagon. Twenty minutes after trading has started, broker picks up breakfast in some hash joint around the corner.

But luncheon—not lunch—is stately. It is partaken of—not eaten—in the Stock Exchange Lunch Club under a ceiling which is 60% gold and 40% silver, or maybe that's the social room which has a ceiling 60% silver and 40% gold, or maybe it's the other way around. . . . You figure it out.

Above the stairway to the luncheon club, a gigantic female, husky enough to lift a truck, embraces a somewhat puny and frightened world. Her blue and vapid eyes are undisturbed by the clatter of a mining drill around her hip. A two-ton redwood stump reposes snugly in the crook of her elbow. Out of her ample bosom, a young man in sweater and slacks sails toy airplanes. Her left hand contains fruit salad.

50

GOLD

Gold has come back. The depression, together with the rise in gold price, brought thousands who were willing to get their feet wet to keep their stomachs full. Large operations were revitalized so that 1938 became the biggest California gold year since the good old days.

The San Francisco Mint is built like a fortress, with sloping walls, upon a promontory of rock. It receives its shipments of the standard of wealth most unromantically. Gold has gone modern. It has discarded the stage coach and the outrider. It travels by express.

Courtesy Yuba Dredge Co.

Gold is mined in four different ways. There is, to begin with, the primitive method of panning. The miner shovels gravel from a river bed into a sluice and retrieves the gold particles which, heavier than the common stone, sink to the bottom.

Hydraulic mining, now almost extinct, forced water under pressure against the hillsides. This method so thoroughly washed the face of the gold country that it changed the topography.

Lode mining is done underground. Since the levels near the surface have been exhausted, this system has come to require large investment.

Dredging is the most modern method. Million dollar engines as big as villages eat thunderously through the gold-bearing flats of prehistoric river beds. The monsters live in ponds, gnawing gravel with chains of buckets weighing tons, digesting the gold, and spewing the refuse out behind.

With the exception of the panner, who remains a free lance, and who, at best, can earn about $2.00 a day, the miner in the old California sense is gone. Miners of the present are employees.

The men who turn gold into money now sit in offices in San Francisco. Most of the large California mines have their headquarters here. Most of the equipment is sold here.

Californians Inc.

Courtesy Rosenberg Brothers

GROWING WEALTH

Farming in California is an industry. Enlarge your scale. Put miles for acres, horse power for horses, and hang a string of zeros on your ideas.

The green things that we eat and wear still grow out of the earth, even here. They are sown with steel teeth, ploughed by internal combustion engines, cultivated by regiments of tractors, sprayed by airplanes, harvested by populations whose home is the current crop, and shipped by the trainload from the farm's own private siding.

California is the nation's market basket. It contains the biggest of almost any kind of fruit and vegetable. With every variety of climate in the thousand miles of state, growth knows no season. The latest improvements added to such prodigality of soil and climate fill the nation's grocery counters, with more than enough left over for export. You can find the empty cans of California peaches (extra fancy) on the back lots of Tokio, Vienna and Paris, France.

San Francisco is the ideal shipping center and therefore the control center of most of this produce. The rich San Joaquin and Santa Clara Valleys are around the corner. Salinas, the world's largest lettuce field, is near by. The earth's biggest artichoke farms and vine-yards are not far away. Orchards of every kind of fruit—with the exception of citrus fruits —grow in the neighborhood. And the whole gamut of truck crops from beans to asparagus are all over the place. What wonder that America's most important canning houses have offices in town. San Francisco is biblical Eve, squared, cubed, raised to the nth power. She seduces a nation with a canned pear.

By volume, fruit drying is as important as canning. California raisins, nuts, almonds, and prunes, the leading dried crops, are handled out of San Francisco.

Most of California's livestock production, which is considerable, and the growing cotton production, which is beginning to rival the Old South, is controlled out of the city.

The management of such colossal properties, the buying and selling, the shipping and packing of such incalculable quantities of human food is bound to turn an essentially productive venture into a speculative one.

The method of marketing, with prices determined at the destination, frequently across the country, and with the shipper paying for transportation, puts all the advantage into the hands of the large firm whose San Francisco offices are in hourly telegraphic contact with price fluctuations. The same condition greatly strengthens the railroads which, from their inception, have played a leading part from their San Francisco headquarters, in California agricultural production and real estate. And finally the San Francisco banks, with much of their investment in rural land and crop, complete the hold of San Francisco over more than half of rural California which in fact, if not in law, extends the city limits over many hundred miles of territory.

Courtesy Wine Institute

▶ Dorothea Lange, from Farm Security Administration

The slums of San Francisco are in the country. In the city itself, there is nothing to compare with the tenement slums of New York and Chicago.

But the industrial character of the agricultural hinterland has created an ever-moving caravan of migrant workers who subsist in jaloppies, tents, and shanty towns. From crop to crop they go, nearly a quarter of a million of them in the state, more than half of them in the South, more than enough of them in the sphere of San Francisco. With their meager households piled on automobiles that would shame a scrapheap, they make a dreary pilgrimage from peas to beans, from lettuce to cotton, from prunes to apricots. Filipinos, Mexicans (those that were not deported), farmers from Kansas and Oklahoma who saw their land blow away, came here with hope—to be caught in the hopeless cycle of the seasons. They face peculiar problems, such as how to keep a family on an annual income of between $200.00 and $500.00, and pay for gas.

Dorothea Lange, from Farm Security Administration

Dorothea Lange, from Farm Security Administration

They also bring peculiar problems. The unsanitary conditions under which they are so frequently forced to live, make these wanderers into a potential threat of travelling infection. Their poverty and lack of expectations congeal into a reservoir of anger, a potent ferment brewing a troubled future.

It is beginning to be recognized that, as long as California agriculture continues to demand a peak labor supply at given intervals in different places, the migrant worker will remain an institution. The Federal Farm Security Administration has established ten model camps where farm workers can live in comparative comfort. Some of the large growers have learnt the lesson. Now there is talk that the State Chamber of Commerce may follow the lead in a big way. If this should come about, San Francisco's rural slums, those centers of misery in the richest land on earth, may be eliminated.

Dorothea Lange, from Farm Security Administration

57

THE PORT

San Francisco Bay is the most perfect harbor on the West Coast. It has everything. With a hundred miles of shore line, protected from the ocean by the narrow Golden Gate, with two navigable rivers stretching far into the country, it has been enhanced by man with every known efficiency device: from piers to freezing plants to dry docks to the world's largest bridges, the world's most perfect airport for the world's largest hydroplanes, and also, the world's most escape-proof jail.

The port is second only to New York in the total value of its water-borne commerce. Regular steamship service connects it with Europe, Mexico, Central and South America, the South Seas, Australia, Africa,

India and the fabled Orient. An active coastwise service supplements the railroads of the nation.

The diverse traffic, with its varied cargoes, makes for year-round activity. When fruit is not travelling, lumber is; when no iron and steel are needed, paper and sugar and coffee and copra keep riding in.

The importance of this harbor, not only to the city but to the whole of California, is evident in the fact that almost three-quarters of the state area ships through it. In recognition of this importance, the port has been put under the authority of a Board of State Harbor Commissioners, appointed by the governor, and thus made independent of the narrowing municipal interests which so frequently interfere with the efficiency of other harbors.

THE EMBARCADERO

In San Francisco, they call the waterfront the Embarcadero. On it you have the choice of being run over by passenger cars, vans, railroad engines, and gigantic lumber trucks which bowl along on what look like stilts, with the driver and the engine suspended in mid-air. Traffic moves at a great pace, oblivious of pedestrians, and will stop only for the trains of the Belt Railroad. These are likely to come clanging out of anywhere, side streets, pier entrances, or warehouses. They stop for nothing.

The Belt Railroad is peculiar to San Francisco. An unbroken link between the cargoes of the ocean to the far points of the nation, it carries its freight, loaded at the ship-side direct onto railroad cars, without further transshipment to the terminals.

IMPORT

Coffee, bones, copra, whisky, pig iron, silk, Chinese wood, sugar, pineapple, sausage casings, structural steel, lumber, cocoa, machinery, rubber, paper, etc. . . . and etc.

EXPORT

Eastward, through the port of San Francisco, the most industrialized nation in the world sends out its manufactures. Throughout the whole Pacific Basin travel our engines, automobiles, tractors, steel, oil. Through this one faucet pours the greater part not only of our handiwork but of our natural wealth headed in that direction. San Francisco handles the

transportation of more than half of California's field, fruit, vegetable, and livestock value which is estimated around 600 million dollars. This harbor accounts for 63% of the canned fruit and 70% of the dried fruit export of the whole nation.

Japan is one of the largest customers. During the last few years, America's broken machinery, rusted rails, and junked automobiles have been leaving San Francisco in a steady stream to become guns, shells, bombs, and bullets.

KNIGHTS OF THE WATERFRONT

Since the big strike of 1934, the San Francisco longshoremen, in a militant union under aggressive leadership, have become accepted as the spearhead of the Maritime Federation of the Pacific, an organization of 40,000 maritime workers from the entire West Coast.

Before the union became powerful and put the San Francisco waterfront on every American front page, a man had to take his chances for a job, from morning to morning. Graft was rampant. The walking bosses at the piers had the control of jobs. You were their friend and you paid—or you didn't work. The speed-up was in vogue. Worker was pitted against worker, nationality against nationality, color against color, in a fierce daily competition.

Now the union controls the hiring hall. Favoritism has been made impossible. A man plugs in on an electric board—and as the jobs come in, he gets his in rotation. No man is allowed to work more than a given number of hours a week. The rates of pay and the number of men required for a job are strictly standardized.

The union has approximately 3600 members. In addition, there are some 500 permit men who are called in when emergencies make the union's membership insufficient to do the work available. It is from these 500 men, and only from them, that new members are admitted to the union, and these only as regular longshoremen die off. The mortality in this craft is high. As many as a dozen a year are able to enter the union.

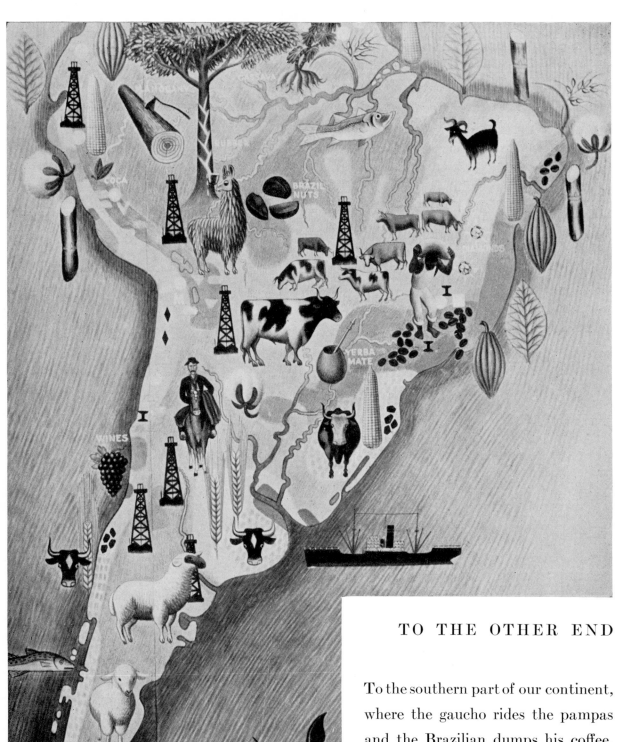

Details from the Murals by Miguel Covarrubias on the Fairgrounds

TO THE OTHER END

To the southern part of our continent, where the gaucho rides the pampas and the Brazilian dumps his coffee, where llamas spit and Indians glide, nudely, through jungles; where ancient cities crumble under lianas, and living cities imitate Wall Street and Montparnasse, Rome and Berlin, all

OF THE WORLD

at once—toward all these places, San Francisco sends ships.

If your longing be romantic, and your pocketbook well padded, you can go in luxury liners to the last outposts of adventure: to the South Seas, to Sumatra, Borneo, Celebes, and the movie colony of Bali.

FROM THE OTHER END OF THE WORLD

San Franciscans are reluctant stay-at-homes. Descendants of adventurers, they have kept a taste for adventure. If the day is pleasant, and one of the big liners is berthed in an open pier, you will see a crowd collect, made up, in the main, of young men. These are not relatives of travellers. They are not longshoremen. They have no business on the waterfront. They come down to look; look and dream a little about the wide ocean that has passed under the bows of the white ship, about islands on the way, strange peoples, and all the romance which never enters an office.

THE CLIPPER

In the Port of the Trade Winds, on Treasure Island, the largest airliners ever built for regular commercial service, land on their trips from China. They fly through the air with the greatest of ease and 40 passengers. The interior of these ships is very hoity-toity. According to press releases, there is a bridal suite with a triple seat built-in settee (we don't know whom the third is for), glass mirrors, dressing table and desk, and an incidental overstuffed chair. Of course, there is thermostatic control, and there are social rooms, bedrooms, a dining room, and everything.

This isn't flying any more. It's living in the air. There is one disappointing thing (to the author) about the new clippers: they carry no baseball diamonds.

One engineering achievement in front of another: the new clipper lands for the first time before the cantilever bridge connecting Yerba Buena Island with Oakland and Berkeley.

FISHERMAN'S WHARF

Imagine a fishing village in the middle of a skyscraper city; a forest of stubby masts with crow's nests the size of match boxes next door to piers big enough to berth ocean liners; the chug-chug of fifteen-foot crab boats mixed with the roar of truck traffic; shrimps, crabs, and lobsters boiled in vats on the street and served, steaming, to the occupants of waiting automobiles. Imagine the pungent odor of fish and rope and tar and of wet nets, the sound of sea boots hollow on planks, the screech of gulls and the dialect of Sicily—that is Fisherman's Wharf.

Every afternoon about four o'clock the sardine fleet leaves for the open sea. In a steady parade of infinitely small-looking white ships they march out, strung across the bay beneath the towering arch of the Golden Gate Bridge. Take off an hour sometime, go out on the span and watch them come at you—there is something valiant about the puny boats, riding, with the great city behind them, into an ocean about to drink the sun. They go in almost every kind of weather. They stay out all night, in cold or warm, wet or dry, looking for the gleam of the schools of sardines that mean their livelihood.

Most of the fishermen are Italians. Drawn here by the fishing opportunities, they have imported the color of their ways and the color of their boats. Especially the crab boats are painted in the brightest blues, reds and greens. As they lie there, in their basin, moored to the pilings of the boardwalks, they bustle with continuous activity. From big, box-like wooden cages, crabs are put into sacks and hoisted upward at rope's end. Boats come and go. Men come and go, clambering up and down precarious ladders and jabbering away. Everywhere nets are being repaired. It would seem that a fisherman must spend as much time ashore crocheting as he does at sea. Against every wall men sit, detached as in meditation, wrapped in the rhythmic movement of the needle through the torn meshes. Along the Embarcadero the long, brown trawling nets for shiny sardines or flat fish are spread out for hundreds of yards.

The sky, the roofs of the sheds, the railings are dotted white with gulls. They watch with predatory eyes. Brazen and shrill, they will dive at your feet for any morsel stimulating to their insatiable appetites.

If you want to do nothing pleasantly, go to Fisherman's Wharf. You will find plenty of company. Somehow the peace and the separate atmosphere of the place attracts those who in other cities might stand around building excavations. Others who prefer to turn their leisure into some kind of occupation, hang a string over the side of the boardwalk. Most of them are "sportsmen"; what they do with their catch is beyond us, unless they put it in aquariums for miniature fish. Another school of anglers is more realistic and more pitiful. They fish to eat. Need has taught them to forget about the bones. These are usually old folk with a tired and patient look about them. The same ones return every day with an occasional novice added. One well known San Francisco author is reputed to have sustained himself in this way for some time before fame came to him.

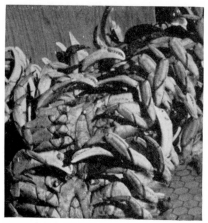

Fresh crab, mister—come in an hour ago. . . . How about some shrimp or a nice lobster to take home for the wife?

If you like your vittles, if the fruits of the sea mean anything to you, if you love your stomach as you should —then put the sea food of Fisherman's Wharf on your must-list. Forget your diet. For once act as if no one had ever discovered calories.

You might conceivably leave San Francisco without having seen Lotta's Fountain. But you will regret forever having missed Olympia oysters, abalone steaks, the tiny native shrimps, sandabs meuniere, and crab Cioppino.

The last mentioned dish deserves special attention. It consists of a stew of chopped up crabs dressed in a gravy containing everything—and we mean everything. It is more than a culinary experience. It is a bath. The waiter will bring you a bib. Don't laugh. You'll need it. You'll have crab in your ears for a week. For ourselves we have re-named this dish: Crab Shampoo.

76

Fisherman's Wharf is more than an amusement place and a gourmet's paradise. Three hundred crab boats, two hundred sardine boats, and a dozen trawlers operate busily out of this fishing port. The largest catch, strange as it may seem, is not intended for human consumption. The sardine fleet, worth nearly ten million dollars and employing twenty-five hundred men, delivers its fish to reduction plants which make soap, paint, oil, and feed mixtures for cattle and livestock. There are twenty-four of these plants in the bay area and several floating ones at sea. Thus—unromantic thought—most of Fisherman's Wharf's old salts are really cattle feeders. It's a new one on us. We used to think cows were vegetarians.

INTERNATIONAL TOWN

San Francisco is as international as New York. But it has a different kind of internationalism. New York, in its beginnings, was a homogeneous town and absorbed its foreign populations late in its history when the immigration waves, attracted by industrial expansion, flooded from an old and overcrowded continent into a new and empty one. San Francisco, born in Spain, raised in Mexico, and come of age in a rush for gold, was cosmopolitan from the first. The village of Yerba Buena already contained all manner and extractions of men. 1848 brought the deluge. The desire for quick and easy fortune ignored boundaries. From the seven seas and the five continents, and from our own East Coast, men came in ships and covered wagons, on horseback and on foot.

Thus it happens that San Francisco's foreigners are not aliens. They give color to the city, and variety, but they know that they belong here, often from Grandpapa up, and they make you feel it.

There are quarters in town which look like little pieces of far-away. Chinatown, Little Russia on Potrero Hill, Little Italy, and, up to a point, Little Japan have imported inimitable flavors of their own. Into the streets of the modern American city, they have brought nuances, sometimes obvious ones such as the gables of Grant Avenue, sometimes subtle ones such as the playing children of North Beach, who, against clotheslines hung with

Monday's laundry, could be cut out of a post card from Genoa or Naples.

The largest national group in town is a pudding made up of so many ingredients that it can be classified only as American. The Germans, the Irish, the English, in all their sub-headings, the French, and the Scandinavians form this composite. They all have their clubs, their churches, and often newspapers of their own; but, in general, you will find that they take more pride in their descent from the rowdy men of gold than their quite possibly more gentle ancestry in a country too distant and a time too long ago to remember.

CHINATOWN

It may be hard to imagine this today—but from the San Francisco of 1849 it was quicker and easier to reach Hongkong than New York. Ready made clothing, provisions, housing materials were brought from China by ships which—believe it or not—took laundry there to be washed at $8.00 a dozen. Inevitably the news spread, of the country across the ocean where gold lay around in the streams. What wonder that each ship, in addition to its cargo of planks and boots, rice and cotton goods and its packages of starched shirts, brought a consignment of emigrants.

Some of the Chinese went into placer mining. A great many settled in town where they were carpenters, domestics and manual laborers. Literally, as they were later to build the railroad which linked California to the nation, so they now built the town.

It was only natural that, strangers in a strange land, they should band together in a quarter of their own and try to recreate the sole environment which meant to them comfort and reality. Thus Chinatown came of age before San Francisco was out of its diapers.

80

The largest Chinese city in the western world is a half way place: not Chinese, not American, with habits and traditions of its own, it draws its inspiration from the old country, its livelihood from the new. Fittingly, the statue of Sun Yat Sen, father of the New China, stands, dressed in old fashioned Chinese garments (made of stainless steel) before an advertisement for tourist trade.

Chinatown has changed. But the phrase, "the old Chinatown is gone," implying that a sudden and unexplained command completely wiped out something which previously existed, conveys the wrong impression.

The earthquake and fire of 1906 destroyed the old buildings; the rebuilt streets look as different from the old, as the rebuilt San Francisco looks different from the San Francisco before the fire. If the California Chinese no longer wear queues on their heads or bind the feet of their women, and if most of them wear white man's clothing, they have merely followed in the footsteps of China itself.

The old conception of Chinatown as a locale of opium dens, tong wars, and hatchet men, has never been true. This phase of Chinese life has always been blown up in America far beyond its real importance by a vicious campaign to create artificially an "oriental menace" for purposes of party politics. In the old days this was especially easy, when the Chinese wore foreign costumes and spoke, almost exclusively, a foreign language. They were deliberately endowed with a mystery they never possessed and never coveted. In reality

Chinatown is a conglomerate of opposites. Not only the American and the Chinese, but the old and the new stand next to each other, accepted quite naturally. At present the modern is in the ascendancy. A whole batch of newspapers, the radio, the stage, carry the Japanese invasion of China, red hot, into Chinatown. Crowds wait for the new editions, listen to loudspeakers bellowing on the street corners from sound trucks parked next to old-fashioned carts. The antiquated clan spirit, kept alive by the Family Associations, is giving way to a new consciousness of unity and nation.

There are two theaters in Chinatown and they are usually crowded. The Chinese go to a show, unless it is one of the rare modern ones, to see, not the product of a new playwright nor the performance of a touted star; they partake in something that belongs to them, like a park or an old temple, which was old when grandfather was a boy.

The Chinese play is a gorgeously decked-out ritual akin to our morality play of the middle ages. All speeches are in a sense, monologues, half sung, half spoken, to the crash of cymbals and drums and the accompaniment of an assorted orchestra. A whole series of gestures, a kind of archaic code agreed upon twenty centuries ago, does away with the need for props and scenery except for decorative purposes. An actor walks in a circle— he has covered a great distance. He steps over an invisible obstacle—he has entered a room. Similarly characteristics of make-up and costume have a definite significance. Red grease paint around the eyes means youth and a sympathetic nature; a chalk white face denotes evil. Long hand-covering sleeves on a man's costume belong to the scholar and the aristocrat; a certain kind of wrist length sleeve characterizes the warrior. An actor carrying a horsewhip is riding; if he carries a fly swatter he is either a supernatural being or endowed with extraordinary purity.

When, therefore, you see an actor with one short and one long sleeve throw aside a glorified horsewhip after walking around in a circle, you can bet your boots that one of those aristocratic scholarly warriors of old China has just arrived after a long trip on horseback.

LOVE ON THE CHINESE STAGE

The gentleman to the right, putting a necklace around the throat of his beloved, is about as close to an embrace as the Chinese actor gets on the stage. The Chinese theater is designed for the whole family and nothing happens which the kids mustn't see. But a great deal is suggested, with a grace and delicacy from which our stars could learn. The audience understands, appreciative of subtleties—not only what it is supposed to see in what isn't there, but what it isn't supposed to see of what is there. The property man, in his old sweater, walking around the stage, is simply nonexistent, as are the other actors not immediately involved in the action, who politely turn their backs (perhaps sipping a cup of tea brought to them by an attendant).

MEETING

PROPOSAL

WOOING

The influence of the Chinese theater is incalculable. An altar behind stage reveals something of the nature of that influence. The fact that the actors are never San Franciscans but are always brought from China, is as significant. Naturally there are other agencies, more potent and less picturesque, which help to keep one foot of Chinatown across the Pacific. The Tongs (the Family Associations), the Six Companies which represent the districts of China from which San Francisco's Chinese emigrated, the various organizations for the support of the Chinese in their resistance to Japan—all serve to keep the bond intact.

On the other hand, as many forces, equally powerful and equally incalculable, pull the inhabitant of Chinatown toward the American way of life. All our mechanical improvements, from the telephone and the automobile to the radio, are bound to have their effect. Our sex standards have done much to liberate the Chinese woman. Our business standards have greatly altered the social set-up.

Most apparent to the eye is the work of the missions, of every denomination of Christianity. Not only churches, but playgrounds and schools are everywhere. It's a strange sight to watch Chinese boys play basketball in the shadow of a pagoda-shaped roof.

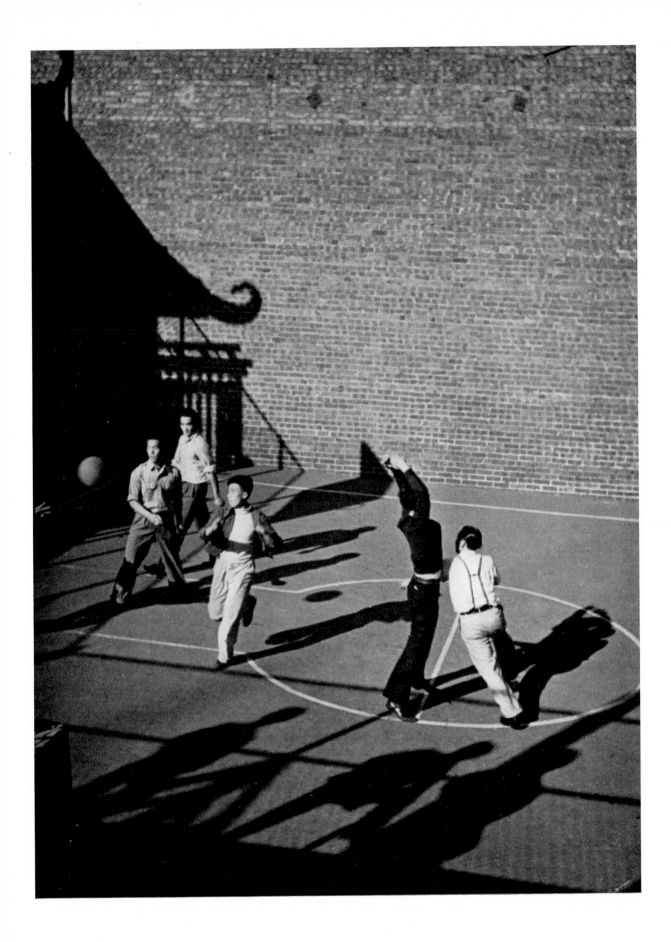

A Chinese picket belonging to an American labor union and a Chinese union meeting presided over by a white woman—those are two pictures it would have been impossible to get a few years ago. The very idea would have been unthinkable.

The change in the American labor movement during the last few years, coupled with the Chinese war, has probably affected the Chinese-white relationship in San Francisco more favorably than any other event.

The maltreatment of the Chinese by the American people and by the American authorities during the end of the last and the beginning of this century is not a pretty page of our history. The Chinese have every reason to distrust us and especially any organization connected with labor. The early California labor movement, through the agitation of corrupt leaders, was largely responsible for anti-Chinese outrages and finally for anti-Chinese legislation. The utterances of Kearney, boss of the "Workingman's Party of the United States," who in the 1870's and '80's capitalized, largely for his own benefit, upon the unusually sharp cleavage between employers and employed, read like the speeches of Hitler, with Chinese substituted for Jews. The Chinese were responsible, according to him, for every evil in California from unemployment to the plague.

Until very recently the Chinese remained ostracized from American unions. Only during the last few years the understanding finally penetrated, that the ostracism of any group merely created a reservoir of unorganized labor. Gradually the union movement began to open its doors to whole sections of the population previously excluded. In San Francisco the Chinese at first refused to be invited. Only after strong resolutions against aggressor nations in general and Japan in particular had been passed in labor conventions did they allow themselves to be persuaded. The new unions in Chinatown are extremely important: they serve as a bridge, effective far beyond their immediate purpose, between two portions of San Francisco, unreasonably hostile to each other before.

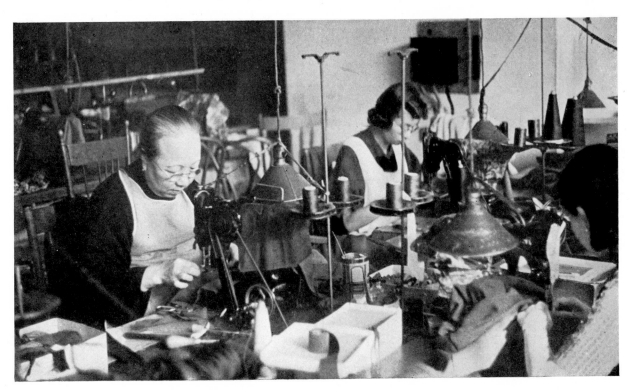

The family is the nucleus of the Chinese universe. Around it have grown up all institutions which regulate the business of living, from the Village Societies to the great Tongs with millions of members; and with it as a center, China has developed a rare degree of local autonomy and democratic procedure.

In America the family has taken on the added function of a refuge from insult and brazen curiosity. The Chinese home is one place into which the casual tourist can't buy his way.

The picture on the left hangs on the wall of a middle class Chinese home. It is a sort of family tree of living (male) descendants made for the eightieth birthday of a patriarch. In the photograph below an emancipated young girl who was born in this country, speaks English fluently and belongs to a trade union, is lighting the window altar for her mother who speaks only Chinese and still sees the gods passing over the chimney pots and telephone wires.

To any commonplace Chinese laundryman or small merchant the continuation of his name in the form of male offspring is as important as it was to feudal royalty. He feels himself as a particle in the current of history and is acutely conscious that the Li or the Chin or whatever his surname may be, has been carried by millions for thousands of years, is carried by millions now, and that it is his duty to contribute toward its continued flow.

On all the streets of Chinatown you will run into the gay porcelain-faced children who may try to sell you a paper snake or a copy of "China Today." Notice how well dressed they seem in a community which is not exactly rich. Off the street, behind closed doors, they are reared as carefully as delicate plants. Their minds which will fashion the future of their civilization are nurtured upon the culture of the past. American kids won't envy them: when they are through with their day of public school they spend another four hours in Chinese school learning to write and read and count on the abacus, and struggling with the tough old classics.

LITTLE RUSSIA

There has been a Russian colony on Potrero Hill for forty years. The Molokani—the milk drinkers, as they were called—are a Puritan sect of peasants, driven from the Volga region and the Caucasus by the religious persecution of the Czars. There are some 2,000 of them.

On Sundays, the older members congregate in their church where they sing the old wailing hymns and the women sit separated from the men. You can get a feeling of what they are like in the hill's community center where they meet to play and learn.

The main body of San Francisco's Russians is more numerous and less colorful. Arrived in the middle 1920's, they came here after the long trek through China and across the Pacific, men of former wealth and aristocracy and their families, to become craftsmen, elevator operators, barbers, and janitors. They live around Fillmore Street, in that polyglot section where they share a far from wealthy district with other lesser minorities.

CHURCH IS OUT

AMERICANIZATION CLASS

LITTLE ITALY

St. Peter's and St. Paul's Church is the hub of Italian Town. Its gilt cross gleaming through the willows of Washington Square witnesses the life story of a people. Italians have always lived on their front door steps. In San Francisco, they live on the Square. Here they chat, wrangle, flirt, and rest. All the daily, small, tawdry and tender things happen under St. Peter's and St. Paul's eyes; and the big dramatic events, the christenings, the marriages, and the funerals of a whole community punctuate the months.

The streets of Little Italy are stamped with the national character. The tall houses, with their alley-ways and courts, and the bay behind them, could be on the Mediterranean if they were made of stone instead of wood. This is particularly striking when, looking in the other direction, you see the skyscraper apartments of Russian Hill or the crowded thoroughfares of Chinatown. It is an odd thing how sharply defined are the limits of this quarter, where most of the 60,000 Italians live. On one side of Columbus Avenue you are in Milan; across the street, where Grant Avenue enters, you are in Shanghai.

Considering that the Italians arrived late in San Francisco—there were only 5,000 of them in 1890—they have certainly made the most of their opportunities. They feed the town. The wholesale market is largely in their hands. They hold a preponderance of the jobs in grocery stores throughout the city. And a great number of the truck farms which grow San Francisco's vegetables are owned by them. In Little Italy itself, there are sausage factories, macaroni factories, wine shops, and cheese shops that sell the imported and the local product.

But this is far from the only function of the San Francisco Italians. They are big in politics (the present mayor is an Italian). They are big in finance (the president of the largest bank is a descendant of Tuscan and Genoese parents).

A brokerage firm from the San Francisco Exchange does a large business out of its branch in Little Italy. There, on the floor, you will find a set of people you would not expect to see interested in stocks. The well-to-do sit next to men who look as though they hadn't an extra five-dollar bill. At the time of the Transamerica crash, the street in front of this office was crowded with shopkeepers, clerks, bakers, and butchers who had lost their shirts. By now they're back again, with new laundry and new hope.

The shop windows of Columbus Avenue are symbols of a national spirit expressed in terms of the commercial. As everywhere else, the Italians in San Francisco have found that local color is a paying asset, and that Italian food is an international favorite.

Occasionally, however, you will find a product aimed directly at Italian consumption. Italian wedding cakes are elab-

orate affairs. They supply the dessert and the memento for nuptials with three hundred guests. The so-called pastries are complicated architectures of sponge cake and icing, costing up to $75.00, and rivalling in decoration the legendary palaces of the Big Four.

The picture on the right is a Christmas scene: with characteristic *naiveté*, and certainly without irreverence, the Nativity takes place, in miniature, among bottles of wine and cans of antipasto.

Among the many native industries of Little Italy, the making of accordions plays an unique part. It does not employ very many people. But its position, in relation to European manufacture, is the exact reverse of the usual: in Italy today, accordions are generally mass-produced—in San Francisco, they are meticulously made by hand, and are frequently exported from here to the old country.

Accordions such as these can be as intricate as church organs. They have as many basses as a leopard has spots. And you can control the octave, the precise quality of the tone and even of the overtones. They cost up to $1200.00.

The game of Boccia, which you see on the right, is prevalent among Italians anywhere. In San Francisco, it is played passionately and, we are informed, often backed by an expression more concrete than mere enthusiasm.

The game consists of trying to place a wooden ball in such a position near a small key-ball that, when the inning is over, yours is the nearest. It is usually played in teams, with two men to the team, who throw their missiles down the alley with skill and virility. Maybe it sounds tame to you. Try it sometime. But be sure there are no windows around.

106

LITTLE JAPAN

Compared with such points of Japanese concentration as Seattle, San Francisco has a small community. The local sons of Nippon live mainly in a few undelimited blocks off Fillmore Street. Quite a number of them, strange as it may seem, reside in Chinatown.

Stranger even is the fact that many of the more wealthy have gained their wealth by running "Chinese stores" on the streets of Chinatown. In the present conflict, this has so irked the Chinese that they have marked their own shops with distinguishing signs.

Japanese restaurants, where Americans take their shoes off and squat, and the Japanese, with their footwear intact, eat with forks at tables, dispense atmosphere, *Sukiyaki*, and *Tempura*.

By far the majority of California Japanese are farmers. They produce vegetable and truck crops, but they specialize in flowers. The Japanese are natural florists and natural gardeners. In their own country, the cult of the flower goes back into early history, and flower arrangement is considered a fine art.

The San Francisco wholesale flower market is a picturesque institution with separate departments for Japanese, Chinese, and Italians. The flower industry in this town is important to the tune of seven and a half million dollars a year. Its product is shipped all over the country in refrigerator cars. The San Mateo region is the world's center of chrysanthemums. And you know that where you find chrysanthemums you will be sure to find the Japanese.

On a back lot near the University of California Hospital, we came upon an event so unusual that we decided to give to it the space we would normally have reserved for the lives of the Japanese.

Archery in San Francisco is a very popular sport. In Golden Gate Park, there are several ranges. But on that back lot, which has been taken over by an American archery club, part of the field is used on Sunday afternoons by the Japanese. Here they practice, in national costume, their old ceremonial archery.

At certain annual meets in Japan, there are as many as a thousand contestants, each with two arrows, no more, to hit, at ninety feet, a target the size of a dollar. Every motion contains the meditation of the East. The archer kneels, before he steps up to shoot, collecting himself into his own cosmos. His eyes are practically closed, his face relaxed, and his movements, as he raises his bow and arrow, are part of him as much as his breathing. Only in the last fraction of a second is he allowed to let his consciousness embrace the target. The arrow speeds—and he stands, listening to the dying twang of his bow string.

In San Francisco, this rite goes on, with only a few participants but with the same solemnity, as though the boys and girls of the American archery club a few feet away, the buildings, automobiles, and trolley cars of the American street, were non-existent.

110

THE LIGHTER SIDE

No American city is better fitted to have a good time than San Francisco. Topography, tradition and equipment are favorable. The facilities are here for day life and night life, for outdoor sport and indoor sport.

The scene above was taken on Christmas day. The Cliff House is the last one of a series which, somehow, have always burned down. Here you can buy cocktails and food de luxe, all kinds of souvenirs and a ten-cent look through a telescope at the Seal Rocks.

A broad boulevard skirts the miles of beach, with the Pacific on one side, an amusement park and a zoo on the other. Make your own choice according to your taste: dream of the isles down-under while the surf rolls in, or win a doll in a shooting gallery.

For a generation the city has been planning a water playground on the bayside, where swimming could be made both safe and agreeable. Finally completed by WPA, Aquatic Park is a streamlined boat on land, with murals, restaurants and every convenience known to human ingenuity. The impressive tower in the foreground is a loud-speaker.

Every Sunday, unless it pours, thousands of San Franciscans cross the bay to go hiking in Marin County. From five a.m. they jam the bus terminal with their knapsacks and hobnailed boots, for the trip across the Golden Gate Bridge.

Their usual goal is Mount Tamalpais, a peak over two thousand feet high. They disdain the road, preferring to test their prowess by climbing difficult trails. A sense of achievement and, occasionally, a view rewards them. More often they look down upon the swirling bay mists.

GOLDEN GATE PARK

San Francisco, crowded onto the point of a narrow peninsula, has preserved its park against all encroachments of real estate. This is the town's playground. It's free and open—not a "Keep Off the Grass" sign in it. At one extremity two picturesque old windmills still act as pumps for water reservoirs.

116

On weekends there are free concerts in the park. Here, between the Japanese tea garden and the aquarium, old and young come to listen to the town band. It's restful with the trees overhead and the beat of old marches and pot-pourris floating off into the blue. There's no pretense of great music. Like all the other institutions of the park, this open air auditorium is designed for the common man: tired from a week's hard work he can sit here and relax with his family around him, and let the music help him dissolve his weariness.

The fly-casting pools are among the unusual facilities in the park. Here Sunday-sportsmen cast with fishing rods for distance or for targets. Some of them are exceedingly expert and place the fly unerringly into one ring after another. A club house overlooks the pools and the frequent tournaments.

Golden Gate Park offers, free of charge, every kind of recreation. There are twenty-one tennis courts, archery courses, bowling greens, children's playgrounds. There are walks over landscaped paths and beautiful drives on which, by car, you can get beautifully lost. There are baseball fields for the young which have produced some of the nation's leading stars. And there are plenty of benches and soft grassy hillocks for the two of you.

One of the kindest and most typically San Franciscan features of the park is a little preserve of benches and tables near the Haight Street entrance. It is intended for old men. They come here, whenever the sun is out, and play chess, checkers or cards under the green leaves. As long as the daylight lasts, all seats are taken. Critical kibitzers occupy the standing room.

THE YACHT HARBOR

Yachting may be a rich man's privilege; boating can be a middle-class pleasure. The San Francisco yacht harbor hasn't a berth open. Next to mahogany vessels of considerable tonnage you will see chug-chugs more appropriately measurable by the spoonful. There are all kinds of craft, from sail boats to oil burners, from cabin cruisers to steam yachts—right down to row boats. The physical culture program of the city's high schools encourages rowing. Crews go out into the bay in sea-worthy skiffs of the lifeboat type. Racing sculls would be unsafe in a body of water 450 miles square.

A CITY LETS ITS HAIR DOWN

You can never tell about a city. Sometimes a passing moment—a parade or a fiesta—will tell more about the permanent temper of a town than all the public buildings.

For the opening week of the Fair, San Francisco stripped off its dignity and put on costume. In that week it revealed itself for what it is—a strange mixture of metropolis and small-town, a business magnate with the heart of a child.

San Francisco built an airport in the bay. This was too good an opportunity to waste. Here, San Franciscans decided, was a swell excuse for a celebration. The new airport was flat enough, big enough, and anyhow, expositions have been in the air for the past few years. So they decided to have themselves an exposition.

This town has always liked shindigs. They have always done them right—with a flourish —noisily, but with seriousness and content not forgotten. So they built themselves an exposition to tell about the Pacific Basin—that vast receptacle for the ships of San Francisco's port—about the history of their home country, about the West and America's Indians.

122

They built it carefully. They built it beautifully. They spent fifty million dollars on it. The week before it opened they went screwy, grandly, collectively, in style.

They threw aside their inhibitions and forgot they were grown up people living in a big metropolis. Bank presidents and cable car conductors grew whiskers. Yes-men of a life-time's standing unlocked the drawer in their hearts where they had kept—securely hidden —boyhood's ambition to be bold bad adventurers. They put on chaps and riding boots and ten-gallon hats and whooped it. They whooped it in offices, in stores, in streets. For a week the whole town played at cops and robbers, cow boys and Indians.

Now I ask you—which other big city could do a thing like that?

This is a picture of opening week. Your grocery boy delivered milk and eggs and canned tomato soup, dressed as if he came just off the desert. Your laundry man was Dead Eye Dick. Every kid in town was dressed to kill—kill anybody he could shoot at with a cap pistol. Store fronts were pasted over with crazy slogans and drawings, and on every second street corner Sourpuss was hung in effigy.

Polk Street became Polk Gulch, restaurants became saloons-for-a-week. Everybody, including the city's dogs wore something to brag of the old West. If you didn't, you ran the risk of being jugged in one of the numerous Kangaroo Courts on wheels into which, regardless of station, a sheriff-for-the-moment shoved anybody who dared to venture out in the clothing of this century.

FUN ON AN AIRPORT

In the middle of the bay has arisen a walled city out of a fairy tale. It is a city where man's achievements stand, removed from the problems which they bring; a city without poverty, beyond the threat of wars, buttressed only against the wind. Crenelated walks, vistas of rare shrubs, statues by the hundred to symbolize a world as we might want it. Gold mines, airplanes, Indian hogans, elephant towers, elephant trains, roller coasters, scientific exhibits, restaurants—all made to look as if to last, all made to last only until the show is over.

Who goes to fairs? Everybody and anybody. There is a fascination about seeing the achievements of the animal called man, brought together into one place.

The San Francisco Fair has accumulated a most unique collection of art. From the China of a thousand years ago, from the Italy of the Renaissance, and from the America of today has been brought this concretion of the human striving for the beautiful.

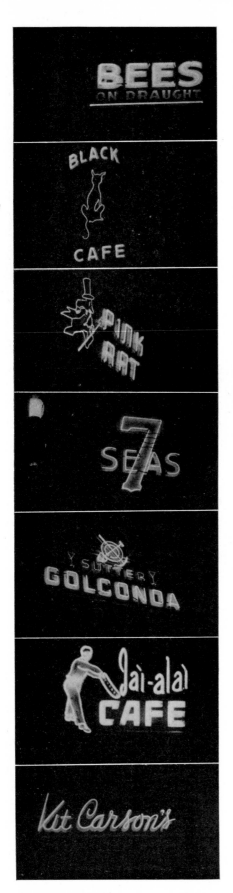

FUN AT NIGHT

Every so often San Francisco gets a conscience. After repeal, when bars, taverns, and beer joints blossomed three times in every block, a committee of the virtuous rose in protest. Result: Signs such as the one at the top of the column in many variations. Beep on draught, Bee on draught, Peer on draught, Puffet for Buffet, Cavern for Tavern, etc. It's done, mostly, by winding tape around the neon tubes. In some cases, such as the one above, a letter was changed. Business as usual.

PADLOCKED FUN

Pacific Avenue, off Columbus, was the stamping ground of the Barbary Coast. In these few blocks, during the last quarter of the nineteenth century, an assorted wild-life such as no naturalist ever observed, thrived under the sign of the black-jack, the knife, the six gun and the garter. This was the home of the "crib" the can-can and the knock-out drop. It is gone forever, its signs broken, its doors locked—though it may reopen from time to time as a rose-tinted chromo of its former tough self.

131

WE SOLEMNLY SWEAR...

Never to forget the cooks and barkeeps of San Francisco. Artists of the frying pan, maestros of the cocktail shaker, they made our stay in this city a gastronomic experience.

Grass mushroom soup, chicken giblets in oyster sauce, shrimps with walnuts in China-town; the *ravioli*, *scalopine* and the salads of Little Italy; the *filet de sole*, the chicken *en casserole* and the *crepes suzettes* of the French; the corn-fed steaks, the thick slices of roast beef in plain American; the sea food—all seem to be a little better here. The wines of California, the convivial Tom-and-Jerrys, the steam beer of the Mission, will always be worth recalling in other places where drinks go only by brands.

The stomach is supposed to be the seat of a man's heart. We have a hunch that in this case it will be—to a large extent—the shrine of our memory.

132

CAMERA LOG

CAMERA LOG

FOR THE TECHNICALLY MINDED

The making of a series of books intended to cover the whole vast territory of the United States presents peculiar problems in photographic technique. In books which use the photograph as an editorial medium the placing and make-up of pictures into the text-page must be done by the author-photographer. The usual procedure of producing only the negatives in the field and leaving enlargement and make-up to the home office cannot be employed. Prints have to be made to size on the spot.

Equipment, therefore, must be adapted to requirements of extreme mobility. For this particular book two cameras were used: A Super Ikonta B with a Zeiss 2.8 Tessar and a negative size of 2¼ by 2¼ inches, and a Leica, model G, with the 50 mm f2 and the 35 mm f3.5. Because of problems of grain and sharpness, the Super Ikonta was used in more than 90% of the pictures.

One of the most difficult obstacles to overcome on this type of job is the lack of a properly equipped darkroom. To any readers interested in photography, this book should be a proof that gadgets do not make the photographer. Our complete darkroom travelled with us in suit cases in the back of our car. It consisted of two inexpensive collapsible enlargers, a Praxidos for the Ikonta and the regular Leica Autofocus machine; three Nikor tanks with a few extra coils took care of the development which was all done by formula in Edwal 12 and Edwal 20. A few trays, a couple of dollar tanks from Eastman's, a standard Eastman safelight, a darkroom clock, a bale of insulated wire and a lot of oil cloth to protect rented bathrooms, completed the outfit.

The film used was exclusively Eastman. Panatomic in the Super Ikonta served for all shots where speed was unimportant. Panatomic X was used in the Leica for similar conditions. Shots of this type are the one of the ship and the bridge on the first text page, the picture of the statues in front of the Stock Exchange which symbolizes 1939, and all views of any distance and extent. Where the subject required speed, we found Eastman's Super XX very satisfactory for both cameras. All things considered, this film has little grain and gives good contrast. The shots in the Chinese Theater of the audience and the performers, taken with no extra light, surprised us by the amount of deposit. The Audience shot was done with a Leica at f2.2 at an eighth of a second. The performance shots were made with the Ikonta at f3.2 at a 25th of a second. There are many shots in this book made under difficult lighting conditions which it would have been impossible to make before the new fast films came on the market. Chinatown, especially, contains a lot of pictures made at night on the street such as that of the little kid and his mother with the baby looking out through the door. These things are snapshots, without tripod. The shot referred to was made with the Leica at f2, at a quarter of a second, out of hand. We're sort of proud of it.

The effect of vibration and "jiggle" is the greatest danger to miniature camera success. Wooziness, blamed on enlargement and "poor lenses," is mostly nervousness and hand movement. We have made a point of using a tripod everywhere we were able to. Out of hand we always shot at the greatest possible speed.

There are no trick shots in this book. Each picture was made to fill a certain pre-conceived space in the layout and to portray a place or an action

135

which, in our opinion, was important to the story of San Francisco and was more directly told by pictorial than by literary means.

Every exterior made in the daytime was shot with a filter. Most of them were done with green or yellow filters (about 2 time exposure). For views and special effects orange and red filters were employed. As these latter filters cut down exposure as much as five times, we were faced, occasionally, with rather interesting technical difficulties. The shot of the Golden Gate Bridge with the spray in front of it, is an example. The job was to get a sky dark enough to bring out the quality of the white ·spray and at the same time keep a depth of focus sufficient to include both foreground and background—and stop the wave. We accomplished this by taking the shot at the precise moment when the wave hung between its own impetus and the force of gravity and thus was, for a fraction of a second, almost stationary. This kind of shooting is purely a matter of timing. If you know your camera and know just how long the shutter mechanism takes to open, you can stop a man jumping into the air at a 50th. This was the exposure of the bridge picture.

Of course, all exposures were made according to meter readings. Many professionals still retain a prejudice against meters, but we find a photo electric cell much more reliable than our eyes. The Weston meter—properly shaded to exclude sky—gave excellent account of itself. No shots whatever were made without lens shade.

A good many of the interiors were made with flash. The picture of the sausage factory in Little Italy is a good example. It was made with a Mendelsohn synchronized flash gun on the Super Ikonta, the bulb being attached to a thirty-foot extension cord and held so as to give indirect lighting. In some of the pictures, we used two bulbs simultaneously, one on the camera, and one on the end of the cord. By varying the sizes of the bulbs, the reflectors, and the distance from the subject, almost any desired light effect was achieved. This operation requires two people unless you want to work with a complicated assortment of stands and tripods. It eliminates the pasty flatness of direct flash.

It would have been a help to have a view camera. But to enlarge out of negatives larger than $2\frac{1}{4}$ by $2\frac{1}{4}$ would have required a machine too bulky for the back of our little car. Closets and bathrooms do not have enough space for such equipment either. We had to make the best of it and get along without rising fronts, and swinging backs. Our ability to move around was most important to us.